Understanding The Bible

Ray Shortell

Understanding the Bible

Citations - Biblical Knowledge

Introduction - Author's Primary Sources

Dedication – Future students

Preamble - Biblical Authorities

Part I: The Power of (Greek) Rome

I – The Power of Rome

II – Removing Jewish Authority: The New Covenant

III – Caesar's Coin

IV – Rome's Authority According to Paul

Part II: Greek Authorship: non-Apostolic Anomalies

V – Dating the Bible

VI – Geography

VII – Ethiopian History (the Queen's Eunuch Treasurer)

VIII – Misquoting Jewish Scripture

IX - Jewish history per Stephen (Paul's authority)

Part III: Theology

Chapter X: Meditation on the silence of Jesus

Chapter XI: Moses and Prophets

Part IV: James v Paul

XII – Cosmopolitan Paul v Jewish James (take one)

XIII – Circumcision (James v Paul take two)

XIV – SuperApostles (James v Paul take three)

XV – The Letter of the Law (James v Paul take five)

XVI – Gospels are Secondary Resources

XVII – Robbing Peter to Pay Paul

XVIII – James' Peace vs Paul's Rabble-Rousing (take six)

XIX – The Family of James (Priestly)

XX – The Family of Paul (Herodian)

Part V: Summary – Final Writings

XXI – The Power of Rome through History

XXII – The Cup of Blood: Wrath or Blessing of Spirit

Post Scripts:

Gospel Anomalies

Failed Messianic Prophesies

Astrology in the Bible

The Teachings of Jesus – the Whole of the Law

Contemporaneous Religions

The Millennial Reign

Apologia from the Bible

Finis: About the Author

Citations – Biblical Knowledge

...much study is weariness of the flesh. Ecc 12:12

...Neither give heed to fables and endless genealogies, which minister questions, rather than godly edifying which is in faith.... I Tim 1:4

...Knowledge puffeth up, but charity edifieth. I Cor 8:1

Many of them ... brought their books together, and burned them before all... Acts 19:19

Quit studying the Bible and go to Church! --Mom ~1987

The church proposes Christ and requires humility and obedience [of Catholics]. In order to understand the Bible [enough to debate the Church], one must know Coptic, Latin, Greek, Hebrew and Aramaic. --Fr Mike, St. Michael's Woodstock ~2007

On seeking understanding

Finally, brethren, whatsoever things are true, whatsoever things are honest, whatsoever things are just, whatsoever things are pure, whatsoever things are lovely, whatsoever things are of good report; if there be any virtue, and if there be any praise, think on these things. Philippians 4:8

And ye shall know the truth, and the truth shall make you free. Jn 8:32

ISBN 978-0-615-92724-4

Copyright 2013 1-1022999321

Introduction:
<pontiff's hat bowed in prayer at cross>

This brief text will redefine the meaning of our Bible. The text will cover when, why, and how its authors arranged the Bible per Robert Eisenman's revolutionary texts, James, the Brother of Jesus and The New Testament Code with additional resources from the Jewish History and Wars by Josephus, 101 Myths of the Bible by David Greenburg, The Age of Reason by Thomas Paine, The Christ Conspiracy by S. Arachya and Linda Goodman's Love Signs. After explaining the Christian view of Jewish authority, the text identifies a few human errors in our Bible to ensure open minds. Then, it discusses the differences between Paul and James. The Bible minimizes the authority of the family of Jesus, promoting Paul's viewpoints over James'. While many have noticed an occasional mystery within the Bible, Dr. Eisenman's Dead Sea Scroll research has postulated a credible hypothesis concerning the relationship between Paul and James, which, in my opinion conclusively proves that Jesus was a real person who loyally went to a Roman cross to allow his family to continue preaching in Jerusalem for another twenty years. Although the message of Roman power or tyranny, Pauline accommodation, and the countering purpose of Jamesian Essene asceticism are missing from the Bible, please note authority as the Bible's primary theme: Jewish, Roman, Paul's, James', and even the authority of Biblical critics such as ourselves. The post-script includes additional information concerning contemporaneous Roman, Mesopotamian, and Egyptian religions with Christian similarities. Dates mentioned in this text are CE unless otherwise noted.

Dedication: For Jake, my young nephew, may you never have to struggle to understand as much as I have, and for Grandma Margaret, who suggested I write a book.

Preamble - The Post Modern Age (the age of no experts)

<scepter and cross with atom bomb>

We live in a post-modern age. A cultural belief in the progression of science defined the modern age. We held experts in awe during the modern age and believed the truth was out there and within our reach. Science fiction suggested time travel and spaceships as advancing the limits of reality, while scientists in white lab coats and black horn-rimmed glasses continually evaluated our progress (1). Since then, we have debunked many experts. The nuclear physicist has had to contend with the meditations of flower children and the discovery that reality is not empirical but existential and relative (2). The psychologist has to contend with the Milgram experiment in which we learned to question the qualifications and judgment of authorities (3), in addition to malpractice lawsuits as authority figures for violating the healthy human boundaries of their patients (4). Philosophy seems at a standstill while people wonder about its practical application. Even priests have been rebuked for anti-social misbehavior, while some wonder why the church refuses to promulgate a proper regard towards civilian authority for the criminal actions of priests with children (5).

However, people struggle with reality's meaning even in our post-modern age. Is there a greater meaning to life? Are we condemned from birth? These questions have gripped philosophers from time immemorial. While some people just try to live a good life, others find solutions in the church's authority. The church, with its long history of grappling with these existential questions plays a significant role in addressing these concerns. The question becomes, does the church bear responsibility for the beliefs it espouses? For instance, recently, the pope has declared that hell is only a state of mind and that purgatory no longer exists (6). Does this absolve the church for the misrepresentation of centuries? Does this absolve the church for the hell-fire preached by protestant ministers based upon their continuing belief of the church's teachings?

The church has a turbulent history, which it seems to be attempting to mainstream. As the future seems to hold the promise of a freer society, it may be considered outside the pale to remember crusades, paid indulgences, and enforced illiteracy (7), but who is to say the world will continue as it has? The church continues to defend the Crusades as a just war due to property considered "stolen" (8). Standard historians consider the Crusaders as murderers, and the church itself notes that mainly the worst sort tended towards soldiery in the Crusades (9). The church suggested such service as an alternate form of payment for indulgence (payment for the forgiveness of sins). Following Paul's encouragement of book burning (Acts 19:19) further inflicted illiteracy on Europe (10). The church no longer wields the scepter of authority, granting itself the right over people to payments for indulgences between heaven and hell (11). And yet, perhaps more is required of the church. Biblical scholars should no longer be required to learn Latin, Greek, Hebrew, and Aramaic to seek the truth (12). If the church wishes to retain its spiritual authority, honesty concerning its origins is in order.

Part I: The Power of (Greek) Rome

In my opinion, all understanding of the Bible must start with the power of Rome. My opinion further proposes that Greek, the language of the Bible, was the Roman language of preference across the Eastern Mediterranean, that Romans considered themselves Greek, and that kings feared the innovation of the message of human equality represented by the zealots of temple worship at Jerusalem (1). Also, in my opinion, based upon the most tenuous connections, John the Baptist (Mt 3:4) and the Essenes (Ch III), like Gandhi, sewed their clothes (2). The Bible and John (specifically) propose true worship as involving renunciation of the world system, which in my opinion, would necessarily include taxes (Jn 18:36), non-compliance with the will of government (money Ch III), and living in freedom (worshiping as one wishes) (3).

I - The Power of Rome

In James, the Brother of Jesus, Robert Eisenman begins by introducing the power of Rome. Rome killed everyone, sparing not even the baby in the womb or child (1). Romans sacrificed to their standards (the double eagle), worshiping their weapons of war (2). The legions tore down the temple stone by stone, fire having melted the gold ceiling into the walls (Mt 24:2). While some lost their fortunes as the value of gold crashed (3), the legions massacred a mere thousand at Masada, enslaving twenty thousand Jews in building the Coliseum in Rome, purchased in temple gold (4). Rome also destroyed those Jews who fled to Egypt along with their second temple at Alexandria (5). Rome has a long history of conquering enemies from Alexander's Greece, including Polybius's Corinth (6) to the Egypt of Alexander's general's great-great-granddaughter, Cleopatra (7). Marc Anthony, known for Julius Caesar's assassination at Rome, also Cleopatra's Romeo-and-Juliette-styled lover (coincidence?), ruled Syria where Christians were first known as Christians (Acts 11:26). When Hannibal failed to destroy Rome after marching elephants and thirty-thousand through Spain, France, and the Alps, Rome sent its armies to Africa razing Carthage. Rome's law reached Marc Anthony's Brutus and Cassius in Phillipi (8), while Paul wrote from Caesar's summer home of Corinth. Israel's history as an isolated and fortified enclave worshiping at the temple was not to last. Claudius Caesar ordered the Jews out of Rome. Rome destroyed the temple along with its xenophobic genealogical temple records and gave the edict that Jews were never again to even so much as look upon Jerusalem (9).

The Bible barely records the murdered millions of Israel (10). The execution of Bethlehem's children would have only been a small portion of Herod's genocide (Mt 2:16-18). Since crosses numbered in the thousands (11), Jesus' request of his followers to pick up their crosses would have been morbid (Mt 10:38). No one returned for the scrolls of the Dead Sea because no one was left (12). Robert Eisenman notes that the power of Rome meant destruction (13).

II – Christianity - Removing Jewish Authority: The New Covenant

Greek "Hellenists" (Acts 6:1) authored the Bible, which is itself a Greek word (Byblios) (1). This text, "Understanding the Bible," only covers the Greek Scriptures from the Bible, mainly authored by Romans who considered themselves Greek, like Paul, who wrote from Corinth of Greece (Caesar's summer home (2)). Roman mythology has the founders of Rome as Greek twins suckled by a she-wolf. The Greek Scriptures are mainly not recognized by Jewish scholars, who continue to refer to "Moses and Prophets" as contemporary rather than "Old" (3). When referencing temple worship, the Christian Bible removes all semblance of Jewish authority from Saducean Zealots, the discriminatory, xenophobic concision of temple sacrifice (works). Paul professed a Pharisaic countering gospel accommodating the Greeks, a decentralized Synagogue worship-centered gospel of "freedom" (faith) (Gal 5:1). Please remember the difference between the Roman accommodating Pharisees and xenophobic zealot Sadducees and pardon this chapter's dryness in referencing each demolished subject of Jewish authority.

The Temple:

Jesus urges Christians not to worship in Jerusalem but to worship in spirit and truth (Jn 4:22 – 24). Jesus said against Jewish moneychangers in the temple, "Destroy this temple, and in three days I shall raise it" (Jn 2:19). The Bible makes a point of identifying the temple as having taken forty years to build before redirecting to the temple of Jesus' body (Jn 2:20). Paul clarifies, noting disciple's bodies as the temple of the Holy Spirit (I Cor 6:9) and refers to the church itself as the body of Christ (Rom 12:15). Paul refers to a new Jerusalem: The Jerusalem above is free… (Gal 4:26). And even the Holy of Holies became available through Christ's crucifixion: "The sun was darkened, and the veil of the temple was rent in the midst" (Lk 23:45).

The High Priest/Scholar/Priest/Rabbi/Lawyer/Pharisee/Sadducee/Soothsayer:

Jesus berates Scribes, Pharisees, and Lawyers for failing to find the truth and preventing others from finding their way (Mt 23:2-4, Lk 11:46,52). Biblical authors have priests saying, "…we have no king but Caesar" (Jn 19:15). Referring to other authorities, Jesus asks whether the blind can lead the blind without both falling into a ditch (Lk 6:39). Hypocrisy, says Jesus, has become the leaven of the Pharisees and Sadducees (Lk 12:1) while those who sit in "Moses' seat" (Mt 23:2) are like unseen graves over which men unknowingly walk (Lk 11:44) (the hidden sin – Lev 4:13). And who steal their parent's retirement for the temple (corban - Mk 7:11). And who wash the outside of their cups (Lk 7:8). Hopefully, you're not confused yet.

From older scripture, soothsayers and witchcraft were killed and destroyed (Micah 5:12). Jesus had nearly the same regard for "learning," preferring some form of mystic knowing which leads followers (Jn 6:45, Lk 21:14, Tim 3:7). Jesus suggests that those who have not witnessed first hand and yet believe in him are blessed (Jn 20:29). And calls his followers children (Mt 19:15, Jn 12:36, Jn 13:33), saying that of such are the kingdom (Mk 10:14) and that neither are the rich to be regarded highly either (Mk 10:24). And not to call another Rabbi or father, as we have one teacher and Father in heaven, and all are disciples and brothers (Mt 23:8,9).

The Sacrifice:

Jesus removed the need for temple sacrifice by regarding himself as the sacrifice. "I am the way, the truth, and the life. No one comes to the Father but by me." (Jn 14:6).

"Whoever eats my body and drinks my blood has eternal life…" (Jn 6:54) "…my blood … is shed for many for the remission of sins (Mt 22:28). Even more ethereally, Jesus does away with the sacrifice preferring mercy (Mt 9:13) and allowing that love is worth more (Mk 12:33).

The Sabbath:

Jesus heals on the Sabbath and argues against the ruler of the synagogue that animals are watered on the Sabbath (Lk 13:15) and pulled out of the pit (Lk 14:5). Because David ate the temple bread, Jesus concludes more ethereally that the son of man is Lord of the Sabbath (Mk 2:23-25).

Food:

Jesus regards what one eats and passes through into the latrine as not defiling the man, but more ethereally, what passes from one's heart through the mouth (Mt 15:17-20). Peter supports this position with a vision of not calling anything unclean when commanded to eat (Acts 10:9-15). Paul follows this up by calling all things lawful (I Cor 10:23), considers offerings to idols as food (I Cor 8:4), but against the conscience of the weak (I Cor 8:10), able to eat anything (I Cor 10:25,31), but choosing not to offend the weak (I Cor 8:13, I Cor 10:28) (3). Note: Pay attention to arguments that double-back on themselves asking to whom Paul directed them (James was vegetarian).

Clothing:
Jesus explains the clothing as ostentatious and hypocritic in Mt 23:5-7 and 13-15, as is commending oneself in the marketplace and from "Moses' seat" (Mt 23:2). Moses' seat would have been the mercy seat (Ex 25:17) found upon the Ark of the Covenant, hidden by the curtain (veil), used by the Holy Ghost and only visited by the High Priest once a year. Actually, Moses' seater would have been a reference to Ex 33:23, where Moses sees the Lord's glory (derriere) [I've heard this as a rabbinic joke] (4). Per Paul, Nazarite long hair is against nature, and men are not allowed to wear hats in church (I Cor 11:4). Paul continues more ethereally that there will be no tradition of not wearing hats (I Cor 11:16), in my opinion referencing men in synagogue who wear hats over long hair in the Nazrite tradition (5). Removing one's hat in church arguably comes from the sacrifice of Jesus as removing shame (Heb 4:16). Nathanael asks about such Nazrites, "Can any good thing come from Nazareth?" (Jn 1:46)

Genealogy (of the priests et al.):
Jesus suggests that rocks have as much authority (Mt 3:9), that stones would cry out (Lk 19:40), and, more ethereally, that Abraham's children would do the works of Abraham (Jn 8:39). Christians don't get that one either. Continuing the stone allegory, Paul explains that Israel, in following the law, the letter of the law written in stone as the Ten Commandments at Sinai (Rom 2:27, Rom 7:2-6), was born into slavery like Ishmael, Abraham's first son, also born at Sinai, of Hagar, Sara's "handmaiden" (Gal 4:22-31). Per Paul, Ishmael represents the children of the Sinaitic first covenant written in stone and deserves to be thrown out (Gal 4:30), unlike Christians of the prophesied new covenant, written in the fleshly tablet of the heart and founded upon "the Rock of Faith."

Jesus also calls Peter "the Rock" when referencing this faith (Mt 16:18), was given the keys to the kingdom of heaven (Mt 16:19) and referenced as the stone which the builders (of the earthly first temple) rejected (Mt 21:42-43), the "Rock" becoming the cornerstone as prophesied, the stone prophesied as an obstacle to Israel (Is 8:14).

Jesus supports children (followers or disciples) as created in belief rather than by blood (Jn 1:12-13). Herod, in an act on behalf of Rome and aligned with the principles of Paul's later writings, burns the genealogical temple records (7). Paul's post-humous writings like I Tim 1:4 and Titus 3:9, argue that genealogies and lawyers lead to fruitless questions and endless debate rather than faith.

Friends:

Jesus stays with tax collectors (Lk 19:5) and commends a centurion (Mt 8:8-10) from the bloodiest league of Caesarea (8). Adulteresses minister to Jesus. The uncondemned adulteress in Jn 8:1-11 is said by some to have been Mary Magdalene, out of whom went seven devils (Lk 8:2). Jesus' friendly banter with the Samaritan woman at the well notes her five husbands while living with another man (Jn 4:1-39). John 4:27 suggests not preventing others from talking with anyone. Jesus feeds table scraps to dogs (9) and Canaanites (Mt 15:22-28) and finds Samaritans more neighborly than priests and Levites (Lk 10:30-37). Now, Israel knew Samaritans as fair-weather kin (10). Note: From this, one may presume the temple priesthood probably kept themselves apart from others (Lev 11:28).

Confused?

Consider folks who only argue Jews are not "Christ-killers" (Mt 27:25). Or that Jesus was Jewish (Mt 5:18 – …one jot or one tittle shall in no wise pass from the law…). And you thought the Christian genealogical debate was only whether Jesus' descent was through Joseph or Mary's father - Mt 1 vs. Lk 3 (11). One other anomaly, that of communion: drinking blood. Jewish law has it that priests spill the blood of the sacrifice on the ground (Deu 15:23, Eze 24:7). Priests do not drink the blood of the sacrifice. The gospels, however, focus on only one portion of the explanation: Life. Lev 17:14 – [blood] is the life thereof…, John 6:54 – Whoso eateth my flesh and drinketh my blood hath eternal life… (please read Postscript: Damascus for more).

The Promise:

The Jewish promise is that in Abraham shall all nations of the world be blessed (Ex 22:18), that no longer shall people be lorded over, "You shall be a kingdom of priests" (Ex 19:6, Rev 1:6). And brings to fruition the following: "This shall be the law I will make with Israel … I will put my law in their inward parts and write it in their hearts" (Jer 31:33). "(To) whom should he teach knowledge? … precept must be upon precept … with stammering lips and another tongue will he speak to [Israel] " (Is 28:9-11).

The promise has been reassigned (grafted into the olive tree in Paul's terminology – Rom 11:17). The Christian viewpoint is that there is a New Jerusalem above (Gal 4:26, Rev 21:2) and that Peter, the first Pope (12), has been given the keys to the kingdom with pearly gates and streets of gold (Mt 16:19, Rev 21:21). Concerning Daniel's everlasting kingdom of heaven (Dan 7:27), in John 18:36, Jesus answered, "My kingdom is not of this world."

The (ten) Commandments of Moses:

Jesus says he came to fulfill the law (Mt 5:17). Per Paul, the law of bondage written on stone at Mt. Sinai is associated with Hagar, the bondwoman of Abraham who escaped to Sinai (Gal 4:24) (7) (Abraham's first-born, Ishmael). The elder is said to serve the younger (Ro 9:12) just as Esau sold his birthright to Jacob. Per Paul, the glory of the first covenant began to fade immediately, hidden by the veil over Moses's face (2 Cor 3:7) (13). The law of stone letters kills (2 Cor 3:1-6) and has become a rock of offense (Peter means Rock) (Is 8:14), while in faith, Jesus delivers us from the law of letters (Ro 7:6). The law of the spirit (Gal 3:2) is written instead on the tablet of the heart (Jer 31:33), wives becoming daughters of Sarah (I Pet 3:6) as we become the children of the promise (Gal 4:28).

This is the end of chapter one. In the context of Understanding the Bible, you should now be aware that the Bible removed all of the authority of the High Priest, from the Jerusalem Temple's destruction (Mt 24:2) down to the temple curtain itself ripping in two (Mt 27:51), from where the Priest operated, what he did (Mt 23:2), how many years he had devoted to studying (Mt 22:2-4), even down to what he wore (Mt 23:5-7), the Bible has its criticism, Hebrew supporting scriptures and common-sense evaluation of why the High Priest is no more than a man. The question to remember is, "Who is the author of the Bible"? Was it the High Priest? Was it a Levite? Was it a zealot anti-foreigner discriminating rich Sadducee? Was it an accommodating rabbinic Pharisee? Or is it more likely that the author was Roman, like Paul?

III - Caesar's Coin
One of Rome's symbols would have been the head of Caesar on Roman coins. Per Jewish standards, the Roman coin with Caesar's picture violated the second commandment against making graven images (Ex 20:4) (1). Artists rendered no images of animals, birds, fish, insects, or people. Based upon Biblical parables and a lack of archaeological evidence, we might conclude that the Essenes and Qumran carried no coins (2), wanting no Roman as their "head." Zealots (Sadduceans) rejected Caesar, selecting one of their own as the only legitimate king (a brother, Deu 17:15) (3). Jesus' command to render unto the temple that which is God's and unto Caesar that which is Caesar's, therefore, sidesteps the tax revolt (Mt 22:21, 2.16.5 Wars, Josephus). Josephus carefully described Romans as honoring the sacred and, thus, reticent to seize the temple treasure (4) (possibly the center of a Jewish banking network (5)). Following the proscription intently, Jesus neither touches coins nor supports the Roman system by working for his coin to pay the temple tax (Mt 17:27 translations). Also, note Jesus neither harvesting corn on the Sabbath as his disciples (Mt 12:1) nor getting his ass out of a pit (Lk 14:5) – following his notice that he has come to fulfill the jots and tittles of the law (Mt 5:17) while ostensibly guiding his disciples otherwise. Pharisaic Paul sided directly with Rome in suggesting paying the tax (Ro 13:7) (6). Per17 Josephus Wars 2.16.5, the tax initiated

the war along with zealots stopping temple sacrifice on behalf of the Romans (7).

IV – Rome's Authority According to Paul

Paul felt that one should be under authority and that Providence set up those in authority (Rom 13:4) (1). Church historians have interpreted this to be Paul's diplomatic acquiescence to the power of Rome. Paul never mentions the authority of the priests of the temple, the authority of the Law of Moses, or of the apostles - only that of the tax collector and his own (2 Cor 10:12, Rom 13:1-8, 2 Cor 5:12) (2). Jesus' claims to authority are similarly suspect, noting both a lack of honor among his family (Mt 13:57) and, John the Baptist notwithstanding, a lack of witnesses. Per Deuteronomy 17:6 and Matthew 18:16, Jesus claims his two biblical witnesses as the Father and the Father's works (Jn 5:36-37).

This is the end of Part I. Chapter I discussed Rome's violent history and genocide in Israel (e.g., temple destruction), which left few witnesses to rebuke any writings unauthorized by Rome. Indeed, Paul's author regaled book burning (Acts 19:19) while Paul rebuked study (I Cor 8:1). Chapter II discussed how the Bible removes the authority of the High Priest's bloody sacrifices asking if the authors were Roman. Chapter Three noted Israel's Sadducean (zealot, xenophobic) hatred for Rome, while Chapter Four pointed out Paul's Pharisaic (accommodating) acquiescence to Roman authority. The understanding is that Rome's vested interest was at least in sponsoring the acquiescent Greek Scriptures as against leaving a tax-revolting priesthood at the temple worshiping a non-Roman deity.

Part II: Greek Authorship: non-Apostolic (non-Jewish) Anomalies

Part II focuses on the Greek authorship of the Bible (the Hellenists). Part II prepares the reader for further biblical examination by covering the bible using outside references: Josephus, Archaeology, Geography, and common sense. Part II proposes non-Israeli authorship after noting misinterpretation/misrepresentation of Hebrew scripture. Part II finishes with Stephen, a Greek Christian, a Hellenist who disabuses the High Priest and gets executed by Paul, questioning whether native apostles, schooled in Tanakh since youth, could have authored these geographical and scriptural anomalies. Also, please meditate upon who Stephen's evangelist might have been in light of Paul's claim to being the apostle to the Gentiles and Peter's future tablecloth vision precluding him as well.

V - Dating the Bible (nativity 7, ministry 37, crucifixion 40)

According to Matthew, the nativity happened during the reign of Herod the Terrible, the king who killed babies in Bethlehem (Mt 2:16). However, Herod of Judea died in 4 BCE (1). Therefore the nativity would have happened earlier. According to Luke, the family traveled from Galilee to Bethlehem due to the tax census of Quirinius of Syria 6-7 CE. Either Matthew or Luke must have made a mistake concerning the savior's birth (2).

The next biblical scene takes place twelve years after the birth with the child teaching priests at the temple, "my father's house" (Lk 2:49 NIV), followed by the start of ministry around age thirty when John baptizes Jesus (Lk 3:23). During the three-year ministry Herod murders John the Baptist (Mk 6:27). Per Josephus, Herod killed John within a few years before 37 (3). The Bible notes that John claimed Herod shouldn't marry his brother's wife (Mk 6:18) but neglects to mention that Herodias was additionally Herod's half-sister (4)! King Areatas, who sought Paul's life in Damascus (2 Cor 11:32-33), is also neglected in the Bible as being the father of Herod's ex-wife! Both Herod and Paul had trouble with King Areatas. King Areatas' army defeated Herod in battle. While Israel blamed divine judgment on Herod's divorce, incest, and subsequent execution of John, Herod blamed his treacherous Idumean troops (5).

Scholars make much of who saw what at the crucifixion. Did an angel sit on the rock at the empty cave (Mt 28:2)? What happened to the Roman guard (Mt 28:11-15)? Were there two men dressed in white at the cave (Lk 24:4)? Why were the women ordered not to touch his body until after the ascension (Jn 20:17)? While church historians make much of different witnesses regularly reporting the same events differently, the unanswered question remains, when did this happen? How might the year of the death of Judas (Mt 27:5) and purchase of the potter's field have been forgotten (Mt 27:7), or ten apostles meeting behind locked doors in Jerusalem in fear of their lives (Jn 20:19 (Judas, Thomas))? How could Jesus' mother, brothers, and sister not remember the year (Mt 13:55, Mk 6:3)? Couldn't the parents of the two robbers crucified next to Jesus be consulted (Lk 23:32)? Or Joseph of Arimathea concerning the year he gave away his crypt (Lk 23:50-53)? Or the murderer set free by Pilate (Jn 18:39-40)? Or the high priest concerning when he made a midnight proclamation that one should die rather than the nation(Jn 18:2,13)? Or Herod concerning when he and Pilate became friends (Lk 23:12)? Or Pilate's wife concerning the year of her dream (Mt 27:19)? How could five-thousand be fed with five loaves and two fish (Lk 9:14-17), five-hundred see the ascension at Pentecost (I Cor 15:6), a person with paralysis lowered in a bed through the roof and no one remembers the year (Mk 2:4)? Couldn't one of the lepers have been consulted (Lk 17:12-14)? Couldn't the money changers at the temple whom Jesus threw out with a whip have been asked (Jn 2:13-17)? How could Luke make a serious historical inquiry and not come up with the day, month, and Jewish holiday of the event (Lk 1:1-4)? If Mark was Peter's scribe (Acts 12:12, I Pet 5:13), how could Peter not recall the year he cried at the cock-crow on the night he sat by three fires while the Sanhedrin debated (Lk 20:50,62)? Could Peter have misplaced even the year Jesus healed Peter's mother-in-law, who then served her guests (Mt 8:14)? Would the family have ever forgotten that date?

Historically, per the crucifixion story, Pontius Pilate ruled from 18 or 26 through 37, and Herod of Galilee ruled from 4 BCE through 39 (6). Lysanias was the tetrarch of Abilene around 40 BCE (7)!!! However, historians record no earthquakes in Jerusalem (8) or eclipses covering Judea or Judea and Egypt ("the sun darkened covering the whole earth") (9). No Roman historians recorded the dead rising. The temple curtain doesn't seem to have ripped in two. No one recalls the High Priest being in charge of Roman guards or setting a watch on any grave. To this day, Christians struggle to explain a savior who rose on Sunday after three days in the earth yet interred only the day before the Sabbath (Saturday). The death of John the Baptist ~37 (10) makes one wonder further about the dating of the crucifixion.

Per Paul, his visit to Damascus was cut short by escaping in a basket and let down the city's wall (2 Cor 11:32-33). After meeting Barnabas in Jerusalem (Acts 9:27), Paul's church started in Antioch of Syria (Acts 11:26) - previously governed by Roman Marc Antony (11) and also church home to Herod's foster brother (Paul?) (Acts 13:1). Paul's famine visit would have happened between 46-48 (12). After preaching in Ephesus, another Roman city, Paul visits Phillipi, where Rome executed Cassius and Brutus (13). Paul's main home seems to have been Corinth, the summer home of Caesar (14), dated by Claudius (41 - 54) and Gallio (50 - 52) (Acts 18:2,17) (15) who per Paul, beat the synagogue official (to me this is major, but Acts minimizes its significance). Paul then returns to Jerusalem to speak with James (Acts 21:18). Paul's stay in Caesarea of Judea would have been through 60 when Festus came into power (Acts 25:9) (16). Paul then travels to Rome by boat, intending to later travel to Spain (Ro 15:28). Hence, per Acts, Paul is conspicuously non-Christian at Stephen's execution and absent from Jerusalem at James' death in 62 (17). Acts also fails to mention the longevity of James, Jesus' brother (Mt 13:55, Mk 6:3, Gal 1:19), who died at 96 in 62 (18). However, Paul's friends in Sidon are mentioned (Acts 27:3) (Tyre and Sidon were visited and dismissed disdainfully in the gospels – Lk 10:13) as are the brothers in three-taverns in Rome (Acts 28:15). Who were these people? Who evangelized them? Where did the Roman church that comforted Paul exist and what was its extent before his visit? Acts neglects the information.

Rome destroyed the temple in 70 and Massada in 73, destroying the second Jewish temple in Alexandria, Egypt, shortly thereafter (19). Twenty years later, in 90, Rome continued the hunt for the Messianic descendants of David in Syria, murdering the grandchildren of Jude, the brother of James (Jude 1:1) (20).

VI - The Geography

<map of Tyre, Sidon, Galilee, Nazereth and Gesenera>

The authors of the Bible seem unfamiliar with Israel's geography. After traveling to Tyre, returning to Jerusalem by way of Sidon would have been tough - the main road was along the coast with Sidon farther than Tyre (1). Mark 7:31 even has the return by Decapolis on the opposite side of the sea (2). Incidentally, the Jewish general Josephus never mentions Nazareth, though mentioning every other hamlet in northern Israel (3). Robert Eisenman suspects that the prophecy concerning a Nazarite messiah implies only a bearded tea-totaller (no hair cutting and no wine drinking) (4). The Bible also mentions a graveyard, pig farmers, a Gadarene demoniac, and townspeople who arrive on the coasts of the Sea of Galilee. Gadara was six miles from the sea at a time when travel meant walking (Mk 5:1). The troupe later passed through the same area (Decapolis) without mentioning their previous "expulsion" (Mk 7:31).

VII - Ethiopian History (The Queen's Eunuch Treasurer)

The authors of the bible seem unfamiliar with non-Roman history, as in Philip's encounter with the Ethiopian Queen's eunuch, who had come to Jerusalem to worship at the temple (Acts 8:26-39). The problem is that the nearest Ethiopian Candace (mother ruling in lieu of a minor son), got defeated by Rome in 22 BCE (1). Per Eisenman, the authors of Acts (circa 90) might have pulled antiquated information from Roman historians (2). Internally, the text notes Phillip's "evangelization" (Acts 8:35 SBL Greek). I'm guessing this word wasn't in use until some years afterward. Dr. Eisenman wonders about "eunuchs" serving a queen, noting this is not the practice in Africa but in Persia (3). Per Acts, the eunuch came to worship at the temple. Per Jewish tradition, eunuchs would not be allowed near the temple (Deu 23:1) (4). Per Eisenman, the entire story may have been a mockery of the Jewish tradition of circumcision, which some Romans considered castration (5).

VIII - Misquoting Jewish Scripture

a) Paul references Hagar as "Agar" (Gal 4:24) and the followers of James as of the "concision" (a reference to cutting) (Ph 3:2). It may seem a small thing, but it makes cross-referencing scripture challenging. Similar examples follow…

b) Matthew cites Jeremiah as Jeremy when Judas casts thirty pieces of silver upon the temple floor (Mt 27:9). However, the reference comes from Zechariah (1).

c) Jesus cites Isaiah as Esias (Lk 4:17), which should instead be Isaiah.

IX - Jewish history per Stephen (Paul's authority)

The authors of the Bible were unfamiliar with Jewish history. Stephen's story of the faith of Israel has a glaring mistake: the burial place of Abraham's wife. Stephen says Sarah's tomb is in Sychem (Acts 7:16). Joseph is buried in Shechem (Josh 24:32) north of Jerusalem in Samaria. Sarah's tomb is in Machpela (Gen 23:1-20), Canaan (Gen 49:31), south of Jerusalem. The question becomes whether Stephen made the error or the author of Acts made a mistake. If Stephen made a mistake, why didn't the author of Acts note the mistake? However, the story of Stephen presents something of further interest, recording Paul as the authority in charge of Stephen's stoning.

Stephen was Greek (1). The question becomes, who was Stephen's evangelist, and why is this apostolic succession never mentioned in Acts 6 (2)? Per Acts, Paul was the apostle to the Gentiles, requiring the tablecloth vision of Peter for authority (Acts 10:13). In Greek, Stephen's name means "crown" (3), and yet his preaching was on the faith of Israel. Stephen was well-studied in the history of Israel for a Greek, excepting Sarah's tomb. Per Acts, Stephen recounted this history for the High Priest of Israel while threatened with death. One can't help wondering if the High priest's thoughts turned to Stephen's uncircumcision. Per Robert Eisenman, some Sicarii, Jewish fundamentalists, required circumcision before allowing the discussion of the Law of Moses (4).

Eisenman suggests that the authors of Acts are brazen. They authored a Greek teaching the High priest who chooses to stand rather than retreat into the temple. Stephen missed the burial place of Abraham's wife without seeming correction by the Jewish mob and without mention by the author of Acts. Wouldn't the author have mentioned the issue, if Stephen made a mistake? Perhaps Stephen's speech should have been recorded more accurately (5). Why haven't Roman Catholic scholars discussed the issue? One final point of interest remains: Who put Paul in charge? What is Paul's relationship with the authority hierarchy? Acts remains silent.

Part III: Theology

"I don't care if there were a few mistakes. The authors of the Bible were people, and people are human!" Mom ~1995

After noting the power of Rome, Part I focused on how the Bible removed all authority from the High Priest's genealogy of temple sacrifice. Part II suggested that the biblical authors were not native (timelines, geography, OT scriptural references). Part III will question the theology of the Bible, asking what qualities you would expect of the Lord and how the Bible might diverge along the lines of Thomas Paine's The Age of Reason. Remember from Part II three meditation points concerning the Greek or Roman authors of the Bible: Why aren't our timelines solid (Ch V)? Who evangelized Stephen (Ch IX)? Who evangelized Paul's friends in Tyre, Sidon, and Three-Taverns of Rome (Ch V)?

Chapter X: Meditation on the Silence of Jesus

Is 53:7 He was oppressed, and he was afflicted, yet he opened not his mouth: he is brought as a lamb to the slaughter, and as a sheep before her shearers is dumb, so he openeth not his mouth.

Is 6:9-10 And he said, Go, and tell this people, Hear ye indeed, but understand not; and see ye indeed, but perceive not. Make the heart of this people fat, and make their ears heavy, and shut their eyes; lest they see with their eyes, and hear with their ears, and understand with their heart, and convert, and be healed.

The gospels would have had a challenging task explaining how Jesus, with his miracles and preaching, might be considered silent while taking on the power of Rome with statements like "heaven and earth shall pass away, but my words shall not pass away" (Mt 24:35). And, "I am the way, the truth and the life"(Jn 14:6). Jesus suggests his only miracle will be that of Jonah being three days in the earth (Mt 12:39-40) and as silent as a lamb before his executioners (Acts 8:32) to fulfill scripture.

Meanwhile, Jesus gets kicked out of Synagogue for preaching that Sidon and Samaria have received the prophets' words rather than Israel (Lk 4:17-30), thrashes moneychangers in the temple (Mt 21:12), feeds thousands with a few loaves and fish (Mt 15:36-38), heals the lame (Mt 21:14), deaf (M5 11:5), blind (Mt 21:14), leprous and dead (Mt 10:8). Yes, Jesus raises the dead like Peter in Acts 9:40. While occasionally asking for his patients' silence (Mt 8:4), Jesus argues with Sadducees (zealots, Mt 22:23) and Pharisees (accommodators, Mt 15:7-9). Do you suppose Jesus could have done such miracles without the acclaim of Israel and the Roman Empire? Instead, biblical authors have the chief priests wanting Jesus dead for raising Lazarus (Jn 12:10), accusing him to Pilate of railing against the tax (Lk 23:2).

Pastors regularly preach the crucifixion and trial. Jesus recalls his multiple previous public discussions (Jn 18:20), rebukes the high priest's servant (Jn 18:23), claims he will return in his kingdom (Mk 14:62), foretells the doom of Jerusalem (Lk 23:28), discusses authority (Jn 19:11) and truth with Pilate (Jn 18:34-38), and despair with his mother (Jn 19:26).

Our meditation is on what constitutes silence: A bruised reed he shall not break (Is 42:3). However, even in the literal sense, Jesus curses a fruitless fig tree that begins to wilt immediately (Mt 21:19). Jesus sees Nathanael's fig tree from a long distance (Jn 1:48) and approaches the cursed fig tree as naively expecting fruit. Although Jonah's gourd grew and died on purpose (Jonah 4:6-11), the fig tree was cursed in anger by one who is said to be our creator (Jn 1:10). Does your creator get angry at fig trees? Even further, John finishes: And there are also many other things which Jesus did, the which, if they should be written every one, I suppose that even the world itself could not contain the books that should be written. Amen.

XI – Moses and Prophets

At this point, my studies were building to an uncomfortable conclusion, and my choice was to pursue the authority of the Hebrew Scriptures:

The books of Moses were an oral tradition until the Babylon exile (1). At least five groups of people wrote the Torah, the five books of Moses. The Jawhist (J) held a belief in a personal deity, the Elohist (E) held a belief in a transcendent deity, the Priestly (P) held a possibly self-serving viewpoint, the Deuteronomist (D) rehashed the previous four books, and the Redactors (R) combined several oral traditions into one continuous story. JEPDR (2). In one potentially self-serving prophecy for Babylonian authors in captivity, Jeremiah prophesizes that any not accompanying those enslaved at Babylon are cursed (Jer 29:16-19). Jeremiah's prophecies for the remnant change as frequently as did his prophecies for Jehoiakim, whose prophesied violent death was peaceful (Jer 22:18-19, 2 Kings 24:6), or Zedekiah, prophesied a peaceful death, who got roasted (Jer 34:4, 29:22, 52:11). In my opinion, similar incriminatingly self-serving comments from multiple peoples authoring the Hebrew Scriptures may be found in 101 Myths of the Bible by David Greenberg, which documents the preceding Egyptian, Zoroastrian, and Babylonian mythology.

Since 101 Myths of the Bible doesn't mention any potential contributions to Jesus from among its multiple mid-eastern traditions and myths, the reader might like to check on other sacrificed saviors, such as Hermes Trimestigeus and Horus (3) from The Christ Conspiracy by S.Acharya. Mithra, the secret deity of Roman soldiers, was born in the cave of the nativity and died on a cross for the sins of humanity (4). Perhaps biblical authors incorporated these myths (5) in addition to transforming local saints into the Christian pantheon since time immemorial (6).

Jeremiah has issues when cursing those who choose to remain in Israel, only to find himself changing the curse as circumstances changed. Jer 20:4 promises the sword to those who don't go to Babylon. 29:16 promises the sword, famine, and pestilence to those who don't go to Babylon. 42:11 begs those who didn't go to Babylon to submit to

Babylon. And 42:16 promises the sword, famine, and pestilence to those who relocate to Egypt. In 43:8, Jeremiah has himself relocated to Egypt, promising that Babylon (Daniel's Nebuchadnezzar) will soon bring the sword. 44:13 promises that no remnant of Judah who settled in Egypt will escape or survive; "only scattered refugees shall return." In 44:28, Jeremiah promises that only a few of those who choose to stay in Egypt will escape the sword, famine, and pestilence to return to Israel.

Note the progression of prophetic modifications. While Jeremiah starts with clear-cut prophesies, in my opinion, the prophet learns and starting with Jer 34:4 as a middle verse gives only the smallest of intimations of a modifier - depending upon your translation, it reads "if you will follow my word" or "yet." The question remains: did Babylon's Nebuchadnezzar ever put the sword to Egypt? After the death of Nebuchadnezzar, Cyrus conquered Persia, and his successor, his son Cambyses, conquered Egypt (7). More to the point, remember that the Bible was an oral tradition until the Babylon captivity. Perhaps only Babylonian rumors claimed Egypt was put to the sword, especially since the deposed Egyptian pharaoh led the armies of Babylon. The Egyptian military had revolted, and pharaoh escaped to Babylon after a loss to the Greeks in Cyrene (Libya) (8). Other major prophets likewise gave similar oracles against Egypt.

While some suggest that the Lord does change his mind (or not Ps 110:4) as was done for Abraham at Sodom when seeking fifty or only ten righteous men (Gen 18:27) (9) or Abraham's nearly sacrificed son Isaac (Gen 22:2, 12), Dr. Eisenman proposes that the authors of Qumran, in my opinion like the Babylonian sojourners, may have changed or highlighted the meaning of pre-existing stories to suit their needs. Josephus notes the texts kept only in the temple (10) and Dr. Eisenman that an overseer like James was the only proper interpreter (11), further proposing that the thousand of Masada spent their final days reciting the near-sacrifice of Isaac at the hands of Abraham (12).

Massada's possible remembrance of Isaac's near-sacrifice makes me question: Regarding Isaac, does your Lord make an evil request and then offer an alternative? In 73, Massada did not give Rome the privilege of victory. Instead, a thousand were felled by their own (13). If Dr. Eisenman is right, perhaps Thomas Paine's Age of Reason might have changed some minds with its exposition on how Moses, the supposed author of Genesis, couldn't have authored his funeral (Deut 34:6) (14).

Part IV: James v Paul (Eisenman)

Part IV presents Eisenman's primary contention: That Paul was most likely Herodian while James, the true authority, resided peacefully in Jerusalem in some form of Priestly service with the goodwill of most of Israel. Dr. Eisenman believes that most of the Bible – the Greek Scriptures - is riposte between these two. When considering James' reticence and desire to keep the peace with Roman rulers, please also note that in Jewish circles, naming one's opponent is not regarded as kosher, and causing another to blush (bringing blood to the face) is considered tantamount to murder. Part IV notes Paul's anger at James' Jerusalem leadership, finds the gospels as secondary resources, and proposes that Rome's motivation remains in stamping out any opposing authority.

XII – Cosmopolitan Paul v Jewish James (Take One)

Per Eisenman, the battle for Christianity happened between Paul and James in the context of Roman imperialism (1). James was known as a quiet man who prayed daily in the temple and was a vegetarian, dying in 62 at the age of 96 while still a virgin, carefully following Jewish law (2). James entered the Holy of Holies, praying for the people until his knees became calloused, like the knees of a camel (3). However, Paul, preaching at all of the Greek cities of the Roman Empire, claims to be a gentile unto the Gentiles and a Jew to the Jews (I Cor 20:21) (4). Paul says at one point he would never eat meat again (I Cor 8:13). At another, that one should not be like those weak in their conscience but to eat everything set before one at the marketplace (I Cor 10:25). Heedless of the table of devils (heathen meat sacrifices (5)), Paul said that all was lawful for himself (I Cor 10:23).

XIII – Circumcision and Baptism: Lawful James v Spiritual Paul (Take Two)

The most significant point of contention between Paul and Judaism has to do with circumcision; Romans consider circumcision to be bodily mutilation (1). Paul was against circumcision. However, Paul had Timothy circumcised to preach in Jewish synagogues (Acts 16:3). To me, this is a significant decision as the rest of Paul's rhetoric contradicts the position, "every man that is circumcised ... is a debtor to do the whole law" (Gal 5:3), "I wish that those who trouble you, would themselves, cut off. (Gal 5:12)". "...Titus ... was [not] compelled to be circumcised." (Gal 2:3). Dr. Eisenman's thesis is that these positions responded to each other, finding a reference to Paul's ranting from James, carrying Paul's point about Jews spying privily on members of the body (Gal 2:4) straight into James' reply concerning the tongue being a small member of the body, yet boasting great things (Js 3:5) (2).

After a six-year probation, James allowed a baptism in the "waters of regeneration" (3), as did the Essenes pending one year (Wars 2.8.7). Acts' pro-Pauline reply, a baptism of "living water" (Song 4:15, Jer 2:13, Zech 14:8, Jn 4:10) was immediate (Acts 8:26-38).

XIV – SuperApostles: Authoritative James v Visionary Paul (Take Three)

Paul himself asserts the authority of James: "Some from James" visit Paul's church in Antioch, after which Peter and Barnabas separate themselves from table-fellowship (Gal 2:12) (1). Paul's description of the Jerusalem pillars includes the words "super-apostles," whom Paul suggests have no more credibility than himself (2 Cor 12:11). At Paul's fifth visit to Jerusalem and James, James has Paul pay the poll tax for four to prove that Paul teaches nothing against the law (Acts 21:22). Per Paul, post-resurrection appearances happened in order, Cephas, the twelve, five-hundred disciples, James and the other apostles with himself last "as one born out of due time" (I Cor 15:9). While James was Jesus' brother (Gal 1:19, Mt 13:55), no scriptural references exist for Paul ever having met Jesus in person.

XV - Letters of Authority: James the Overseer v Paul the Pontificator (Take Five)

Dr. Eisenman suggests that James certified teachers with a letter of recommendation (1). Robert Eisenman spends much time meditating on Paul's rhetoric against the letter of the law: Paul explains that he does not need letters - that church members have his letters of credibility written in their hearts (2 Cor 3:3). Paul continues explaining that the church should be vouching for his credibility in such a way that Paul need not argue further (2 Cor 12:11). Paul argues that the letter of the law brings death (2 Cor 3:6).

XVI - Gospels are Secondary Resources

It is well known that Paul's writings pre-date the gospels. Historians suggest the authors delayed writing the gospels, believing the second coming imminent. The argument suggests they wrote the gospels much later, when the remaining authors had reached old age (1).

XVII - Robbing Peter to pay Paul

This metaphor, whose origins have been lost to time, speaks volumes about the relationship between Peter and Paul (1). Dr. Eisenman suggests that Peter was a Jewish, law-abiding, orthodox zealot whose authority was overwritten by the authors of the Bible (2). You'll remember it was Peter Jesus rebuked as Satan in the gospels (Mk 8:33), sank in the sea for lack of faith (Mt 14:29-31), and failed three times to identify himself as a disciple (Mk 14:72). Peter's three declarations of love end the gospel of John (Jn 21:15-17).

Per Acts 12:17-19, Peter's escape from prison results in the death of his guard and flight from Jerusalem. On the other hand, Paul chooses not to flee and converts his guards (Acts 16:28) (3). Without an explanation for Peter's return from banishment, Peter speaks at the Jerusalem council (Acts 12:3-4,17-19, Acts 15:1-29) (4) on behalf of Paul, saying that the law is too hard for himself or any previous Jews to bear (a bit of an odd statement, Acts 15:10).

While James wields his authority quietly, Paul regularly boasts (5), supported, or justified with visions (Acts 9:3 – Road to Damascus). Per Acts, Peter has one similar vision: Peter's tablecloth drops three times (Acts 10:10-16), linking it to other instances where Peter is found "weak in the faith" (6). The vision is a direct contradiction to Jewish dietary laws and is used to promote Paul's ministry to the unclean (gentiles). Dr. Eisenman notes Jesus' Christian dietary requirements (Mt 15:17), showing that Peter somehow missed this lesson during Jesus' lifetime (7).

XVIII – Jerusalem: Peaceful James v Rabble-Rousing Paul (Take Six)

James, a lifelong virgin, resided peacefully in Jerusalem among his kindred (1). James had strained relations with Rome, and authorities had him thrown down the temple steps around 40 and stoned to death following the same in 62, the suggestion being these somehow related to Paul's visits (2), bookended by the sacrifice of Jesus and destruction of the temple. James' brother, sometimes called "Simon bar Clopas," lived for many years afterward, reputedly dying a vegetarian at 120 (3). James had little to say negatively against anyone (Ja 1:19). Extra-biblical references call James "the Just one," who could interpret the scriptures and prophets (4), much as Jesus was said to have done on the temple steps at the age of twelve (Lk 2:42-47).

However, any of Paul's visits to Jerusalem reportedly involved uprisings by the general populace against Paul (5). Per Acts, James tries to get Paul in and out quietly. However, Paul's nephew needs to speak to the captains of the Roman guard to prevent Paul's death in one instance (Acts 23:16-22). While Galatians reports a quiet visit after Paul's conversion and stay in Damascus (Gal 1:18-19), Acts reports the same visit to Jerusalem as beset by rabble-rousers (Acts 9:29).

XIX - The Family of James (Priestly)

How many apostles are in the Bible? Can you name them? The biblical lists of the apostles are different (Mt 10, Lk 6). Dr. Eisenman suggests that the twelve mainly consisted of the four brothers of Jesus, of whom James would have been foremost. The four brothers of Jesus were James, Simon, Joses, and Judas (Mt 13:55, Mk 6:3). Per Dr. Eisenman, each may have had two stand-ins amongst the apostles, for example, James the Greater and James the Less (Mk 15:40) (1), such dissimulation leading to the many Marys within the Bible, even one Mary, the sister of Mary (Jn 19:25) (2).

James is mentioned in the lists of the apostles twice as James the son of Alphaeus (Mt 10:3), James son of Zebedee (Mt 10:3), and James the less (Mk 15:40). Per Acts, the original James is "put to the sword" (Acts 12:2), after which the more well-known James makes his appearance without introduction as if we are supposed to have already understood his significance (3). James was famous as the leader of the Jerusalem assembly, as discussed in Josephus Antiquities 20.9.1.

Simon is likewise mentioned several times in the lists of the apostles as Simon, Simon the zealot, Simon Peter (Mk 10:2-4), or even Simeon (Acts 14:5) (4).

Judas is mentioned in the gospel lists in multiple variations too: Jude (Jude 1:1), Judas, the brother of James (Acts 1:13), Thaddeus (Mk 3:18) or Lebabus (Mt 10:3), Theudas (no vowels in Hebrew, Acts 5:6) and Judas Iscariot (Lk 6:16). Dr. Eisenman even notes Mark's "Andrew" as having an overwrite in the gospel of John with Simon Peter's Thomas Didymus (Jn 21:2, 5). Dr. Eisenman notes that Thomas means "twin" in one language, while "Didymus" likewise means twin in another (6). The apocryphal gospel and acts of Thomas (Judas Thomas (7)) note that at one point, Thomas is mistaken for Jesus (8). Dr. Eisenman suggests Judas Thomas (Judas, Thaddeus, Jude) as the twin of Jesus (9).

Per Dr. Eiesnman's linguistic studies, there is but one vowel separating the fourth brother, Joses, from the subject of the gospels, Jesus (10). Hmm.

Twelve elders and three priests ruled James' Essene community (11). Per Dr. Eisenman, we cannot currently determine whether the three priests were part of the twelve or separate (12). Rulers of this community, who escaped into the desert and the homeland of Abraham, may have included the family of Jesus (13). As a linguist, Dr. Eisenman suggests that, similarly to other words crossing languages, Iscariot was a mix-up of the name Sicarii. These knife wielders promised to forsake eating until killing Paul (Josephus 20.8.10, Acts 23:12). Dr. Eisenman suggests these as using their curved knives for circumcision (14), equating these words: Sicarii, Iscariot, Zealot, Sadducee, and Jewish-Christian.

XX – The Family of Paul (Herodian)

Dr. Eisenman makes the case that Paul was of the family of Herod (1). Rome controlled the High Priest's vestments (clothes) (2). Both Paul and Herod disagreed with King Areatas (Chap V). Per Josephus, a particular nephew named "Saulos" traveled, visiting many places named in Acts (3). Per Acts, Paul was in charge of Stephen's stoning on behalf of the temple priests (Acts 7:58). Per Acts, Paul's nephew calls the captain of the guard from Caesarea to protect Paul (Acts 23:16). Per Acts, Paul's church in Antioch, where Christians were first called Christians (Acts 11:26) lists as one member, Manaen, a foster brother of Herod (Acts 13:1). Paul himself notes his Roman citizenship as being of "no mean city" (Acts 22:25, Acts 21:39) (Paul's family). Paul's churches all started in Roman-controlled cities, and Paul's last wish is to visit Spain (Rom 15:28), the country of origin of his Roman rulers of Corinth (5). Dr. Eisenman notes Paul's seeming "light house arrest" under many of his Roman guards and nephew and sister in Rome (4) while being "mobbed" in Jerusalem (6). Paul regularly sides with Rome on points of law while finding the Jewish law to have little, if any, practical merit (circumcision and dietary laws). Finally, in addition to suggesting Paul's fellow worker Epaphroditus (Ph 2:25) as Josephus' sponsor (7), Dr. Eisenman notes Paul's reference to his "kinsmen" in Rome, including "the littlest Herod" (Ro 16:11).

As for Paul's relations in Antioch, Jerusalem, Arabia, and possibly Turkey – "All in Asia have abandoned me" II Tim 2:15.

This is the end of part IV. Per Dr. Eisenman, Paul's witness has been compromised by Roman affiliations while James teaches peacefully in Jerusalem. Meanwhile, the gospels ruthlessly undermine the authority of Jesus' family (Judas, Peter, James, and Joses) along with his parents and sisters (Mt 12:48, 19:29).

Part V: Summary
XXI - The power of Rome through History
Dr. Eisenman suggests that the Messianic movement in Israel was the most critical threat to Rome and focused on not paying taxes (1). Therefore, the gospels put James's family into disrepute. Hence the overwriting of names (2), changing of doctrines (3), and usurpation of religion. The millions of Jews murdered in this Roman military, political, and religious operation have unfortunately carried through thousands of years into the Holocaust. Dr. Eisenman's research further shows that James's teachings underpin Islam's religion of Abraham (4).

This text, Understanding the Bible, is packed with information anomalous for nearly two millennia. It is brief, written for those without the time to pore over tons of material, which those in Authority (Roman Catholic Priests) tell people we must do before disputing with the Church (5). The church has its method of handling this possibility, too: Don't enjoin doubtful disputations (Ro 14:1). Serious study quickly reveals many biblical references encouraging ignorance, burning books (Acts 19:19), castigating the lettered (pun intended to include both the letter of the law and lawyers per Paul and gospels), and noting the cost of study (6).

While many like Thomas Paine have noticed the occasional anomaly, Dr. Eisenman has put together a comprehensive analysis ensuring that the Jamesian tradition of works, as opposed to the Pauline position of faith, will be recognized by more than Latter-Day Saints. Mormons preach works (7) and exclude black sheep (8). In Dr. Eisenman's work, James comes to life as a reliable witness to peace. I believe that the family of James, as leaders in Jerusalem, allowed the sacrifice of Jesus in some form of proof of loyalty to Rome, which later turned into the Catholic doctrine of humility and obedience (9) … consider that is expedient for us, that one man should die for the people and that the whole nation perish not (Jn 11:50). After Jesus' sacrifice, James was allowed to continue in Jerusalem another couple of decades, even wearing the mantle of High Priest and praying in the Holy of Holies (10).

XXII - The cup of Blood: Wrath or Blessing of Spirit
One code word mentioned by Dr. Eisenman is "Damascus." In Hebrew, Chos means cup, as in `cup of wrath` (Jer 25:15) (1) spilled forth upon the earth in the day of the Lord (Rev 14:10). Dam refers to blood, as in `upon the rivers of Egypt` (Ex 7:19). For the Essenes (whether Jessaeans, or Zadokite Sadducees, Zealots, Nezer Nazrites, Sicarii or Jewish-Christians per Eisenman(2)), Damascus was merely the new covenant – a rededication to the Abrahamic covenant of circumcision (Gen 17:14, recall Moses' wife's reference to the ceremony as "bloody" Ex 4:25). Not so for the Rabbinic Roman-accommodating Pharisees (3) and for similarly Roman-accommodating Paul, it was the cup of the blood of Christ (4). Per Dr. Eisenman, much of the Biblical text follows Qumran documents metaphor for metaphor, changing one and reversing another (5): Paul's relation of drinking "the cup of blessing" appears but once outside of the Gospels, which were written much later (I Cor 10:16) (6).

In Jewish sacrificial ceremonies, the meat was eaten, but blood was always spilled on the ground or sprinkled on the altar, priest, or people (Deu 15:23, Lev 8:24,30, Ex 8:28). Paul relates the mystery of the bread of the body and cup of blood as received from the Lord (I Cor 11:20-26), presumably the breaking of bread from Antioch (Acts 20:7 - Macedonia), which is interesting since Paul fusses incessantly against James' authority (Gal 2:6, 9) (Jesus' brother (7)), never met the Lord in person, having previously persecuted the church (Acts 22:4, 7:58) and only gives the most sparse of details regarding his visions (Acts 22:7-9). 1 Cor 11:21, Acts 2:3, and Eph 5:18 mention disciples getting drunk, meaning Paul's cup of blood and blessing was wine.

Per Dr. Eisenman, `Greek` and `wine` sound the same in Hebrew (8). Wind (Ruach) is also spirit or the breath of life, much the same as spirits can refer to alcohol or liveliness in English. And branch (of the vine Jn 15:5) is similar to "holy," or "keeper of the covenant." Therefore, wine refers to Hellenists, whose mystery cults had as their preoccupation the conquest of death (9) awaiting Jesus' arrival on the winds of heaven (clouds). Therefore, the "well of living waters" (10) (Jn 4:10) becomes wine through Jesus at the wedding (Jn 2:7-9), which grafted in the Gentiles (Greeks) (Rom 11:17) (11). Jesus' allusion to his being the "vine" would be "grapes," "wine," or "Greek," and we, the "branches" would be "keepers of the covenant," and "holy" "spirits" (Jn 15:5 (12)). With these new wineskins (Lk 2:22 NIV), foreskins (13), or "Greek Keepers of the covenant" introducing uncircumcised gentiles into the temple, is it any wonder the trouble around Paul in Jerusalem?

On the opposite side, noted though centuries in the Dead Sea Scrolls unedited by Rome, Jewish Christian (Sadduceen = Zealot) Jamesian followers had some choice adjectives for accommodating pharisaic Paul as well: church built on blood, empty cup, windbag, liar or empty man (14). Per our discussion above, windbag references both spirit (wind) and sacrifice (skins, bag). Throughout history, Rome utterly destroyed this alternative interpretation. For example, Paul's Lucan author noted book burnings in Acts 19:19. Paul requested pity rather than anger from others in I Cor 15:19 (15). As Paul stated in II Tim 1:15, "This you know, that all those in Asia have turned away from me," which means everywhere east of Greece, the church had abandoned Paul. (16)

Postscript: Gospel Anomalies

If all of the preceding is true, that James and Paul had a running dispute, that Paul's writings predated the gospels, that Rome was using the gospels and Acts to overwrite religious elitists who used Mecca-like warning-markers to bar foreigners from the Inner Courtyard of the Temple on pain of death (1), then the philosophy of the gospels would necessarily show human, rather than heavenly contradictions. Here are a few:

1) Jesus says his time is not yet here, not to be revealed, that even Elijah and Moses' testimony couldn't convince others of Jesus' mission, that people can listen but not hear, and that this generation will have no sign… before healing the lame, deaf, blind, palsied, dead, lepers and demon possessed, stampeding pigs, turning water into wine, whipping moneychangers at the temple, being born under a star, given gold, frankincense and myrrh by kings, baptized by John with a voice from the sky and descent of the Holy Spirit like a dove or tongue of fire from the heavens, talking with Moses and Elijah, face shining radiantly on a mountain top while listening to a voice from the clouds, seeing Nathaniel under a tree, sending disciples on a specific mission for an ass and foal tied to a tree, telling a Samaritan about her living arrangements and being called a prophet, having bad fishers fill their nets to nearly breaking with a haul from the other side of the boat, calming the sea, walking across water and into town on the foal of an ass across palm fronds, cursing a tree which shortly dies, flying into heaven, and feeding thousands with a couple of fish and five loaves of bread (technically flying into heaven happened after the crucifixion).

2) After suggesting turning the other cheek (Lk 6:29), Jesus heals the ear of Malchus, the

servant of the high priest (Lk 22:51). Peter, castigated Peter, had cut off Malcus' ear (Jn 18:10). Jesus had previously asked his followers to carry swords (Lk 22:36).

3) Another contradiction concerns unbelievers. At one point, Jesus explains that those who are not against us are with us (Lk 9:50). Two chapters later, those who are "lukewarm" and those who are not with Jesus are against him (Lk 11:23, Rev 3:16).

4) Yet another contradiction has to do with teachers. The parable of the lamp under a basket suggests teaching good things (Lk 8:16). The parable of pearls before swine suggests withholding information from those who wouldn't find value (Mt 7:6).

5) Another scriptural goof comes in per Dr. Eisenman's "blood libel." Per Scripture, Jerusalem has killed the prophets sent to her, which some have held against Israel ever since (although a Sanhedrin required 70 judges, the Essene trial was by 100 (Wars 2.8.9)). Dr. Eisenman notes Israel as killing very few prophets: Jeremiah was not killed, although generally unliked for his prophecies against Jerusalem concerning the Babylonian exile (Jeremiah) (2).

Perhaps the worst example of unloving behavior, however, has to do with the Roman view of Jews. The gospel authors dehumanized "the Jews". Some priests might wonder at why all Jerusalem supposedly turned out for Palm Sunday, followed shortly by all the Jews requesting a crucifixion (3). The question becomes how many would have represented the entire people – per Mk 15:43, one Joseph of Arimathea of the Sanhedrin was certainly not present. The Sanhedrin consisted of seventy elders (JewishRoots.net). In a time of chariots and lack of a printing press, most would have been scattered throughout Israel and unaware of the proceedings. Rabbis report it would have been illegal for the Sanhedrin to have convened in the manner described (4). Enlightened Christians have long noted the power of Rome when explaining how the gospels feverishly attribute the cause of the crucifixion anywhere except Rome. For two thousand years a persecuted people have maintained their innocence, which the pope has recently supported (5).

Postscript: Failed Messianic Prophesies

Context: …ye know in all your hearts and in all your souls that not one thing hath failed of all the good things which the LORD … spake concerning you; all are come to pass unto you, and not one thing hath failed therof.   Jo 23:14

Jeremiah 33:17: For thus saith the Lord; David shall never want a man to sit upon the throne of the house of Israel;

Genesis 49:10: The scepter shall not depart from Judah, nor a lawgiver from between his feet until Shiloh come; and unto him shall the gathering of the people be.

To me, the prophecy failed during the Babylonian captivity: The king was hauled off to a dungeon in a foreign country and later lived at the table of the Babylonian king. The scepter had departed. The next discredible prophecy to me concerns the lost ten tribes of

Israel. These left Israel due to the human slavery of Judah (1) or invasion by Assyria (II Kings 16:9). In memoriam, Israelis were renamed Jewish, because of the twelve tribes, effectively only Judah remains. To me, the promise doesn't hold if folks leave, are wiped out, or can no longer reliably trace a remnant to each of the twelve tribes (Judges 21:6,15,17). How can the scepter remain if the subjects depart? Jeremiah's prophecies fail, too. First, anyone who doesn't go to Babylon will die (Jer 20:4). Next, Jeremiah begs the remaining folks not to flee to Egypt, or they will die (Jer 24:8-10, Jer 29:16-18). Finally, Jeremiah explains that those in Egypt will die (Jer 44:27), and only a few will return from Egypt (Jer 44:28).

Dr. Eisenman even questions the genealogy of the High Priests before Herod (2).

Postscript: Astrology in the Bible

In my opinion, Paul's most beautiful and well-known writing, indeed Paul's sole positive spiritual contribution, unlike the rest of his eat anything and do everything because life is short (Lk 12:29-34)), is the Love chapter of 1 Cor 13, which was originally authored by astrologers in the mythology of Hercules' twelve tasks. Per "The Christ Conspiracy" by S. Arachya 1999 pg113, Saul's hometown, Tarsus of Galatia, annually re-enacted the myth, which ends in burning the body of the hero. I Cor 13's secret is starting with Taurus rather than Aries and combining Capricorn and Aquarius into one statement: Love rejoices not in Evil but rejoices in the truth. Review the book, Linda Goodman's Love Signs, page 13, for 1 Cor 13 qualities using similar words (1).

As one of the few esoteric sciences at the time, Astrology was deeply embedded along with reincarnation into some Jewish sects (2), as may be found today when studying Kaballah. Another intertwining of Astrology into the Bible comes through Paul's discussion of a man he knew who visited the third heaven (2 Cor 12:2). Per writings extant from that time, the book of Enoch describes the seven heavens, which were associated with the seven visible "planets" from Astrology - Sun, Moon, Mercury, Venus, Mars, Jupiter, and Saturn. Saturn was considered the furthest sphere of the heavens, the "seventh" heaven. Likewise, per Josephus, a concurrent author for Rome who was an ex-patriot of Israel in the "Jewish War," the temple itself represents of the earth, the oceans, and the third, hidden part behind the curtain represents the heavens (3).

Postscript: The teachings of Jesus – the Whole of the Law

For those who note Jesus' erudite rendition of the law as a positive contribution in Mt 22:39, Mk 12:31 & Lk 10:27, *"Love the lord your G-d with all your heart, soul, strength, and might, and love your neighbor as yourself,"* this postscript cross-references Hillel who had previously taught the whole of the law while standing on one foot, *"Thou shalt not do unto others what you would not have them do unto you; the rest is commentary, now go and study."* Hillel's grandson, Gamaliel, was a teacher of Paul (Acts 22:3), and Paul's letters predate the gospels (Ch XVI Gospels are Secondary Resources). James 2:8 also references this royal law according to scripture (1) in Lev 19:18 and Deu 6:5 <below>.

Deu 6:4-5 Hear, O Israel: The Lord our G-d is one Lord: And thou shalt love the Lord our G-d with all thine heart, and with all thy soul, and with all thy might.
Lev 19:18 ...thou shalt love thy neighbor as thyself...

Postscript: Hebrew Bible issues

The Hebrew Bible has several discrepancies. 101 Myths of the Bible documents these best in terms of the Egyptian creation myths. Other standard refutations include the ancient Hebrew belief in a flat world (Is 45:6), the four winds (Jer 49:36) or angels (Rev 7:1), the sun standing still for "the whole earth" (Josh 10:12-13) or tower of Babel built up unto heaven (Gen 11:4). In addition to prophets missing their mark (Daniel misses his current king (1) and Jeremiah's prophesies get modified more and more (2)), oddities include describing the camel as not cloven-hoofed (Lev 4:11), insects as having only four feet (Lev 11:21-22), and not allowing garments of both wool and linen (Deu 22:11) (symbolically eschewing racial intermarriage (3)). Wool comes from an animal that reproduces via intercourse, thereby making linen the priestly choice (Ez 44:17).

Postscript: Contemporaneous religions
From Zoroastrianism, which was likewise heavily into Astrology, we get the metaphor of an angel of light whispering into our right ear and the devil whispering into our left. Per Zoroastrianism, two "gods" battled for eternity. The good won, confining the evil to "time." While this deity has current reign over us, the "good god" has written the final chapter (1). Ergo the devil, prince of the power of the air (Eph 2:2), could offer Jesus all the worldly kingdoms (Mt 4:8).

From the Egyptian mysteries comes Osiris, a solar deity who, each winter, "dies" for three nights. The sun reaches its lowest point in the day sky until reborn by beginning its northward travels. This annual resurrection was said to have been mediated by Osiris' virgin mother Isis (2). Additionally, Hebrew Scriptures regularly mention the Babylonian and Chaldean astrologers (Dan 5:7). Job's "Mazzaroth" (Job 38:32) could have been replaced by the English "Zodiac" as Paul's masthead of "Dioscuri" or "heavenly twins" should have been replaced by "the twins of Gemini" (Acts 28:11).

Postscript: The Millennial Reign
Dedicated to the millennia of research and progress humankind could have made in the sciences and philosophy were it not being fed 'benevolent' spiritual milk (I Cor 3:2). And to my young nephew, Jake Kernan, may you never need to similarly dedicate yourself to years of study to find the truth which sets one free (Jn 8:32) (1) (although the authors might have preferred 'in your face!'). And to those whose feelings alone lead to inspirational and hard-won convictions (Courtney Williams, Sidelines Kennesaw, GA '08), may our studies and beliefs support each other.

Final Note:
Were this true, wouldn't the church have pre-set in scripture the actions believers were to take in the face of such evidence? Since the Bible defines these actions, does this mean

that its authors were aware of these potential concerns? Would having a plan for followers support evidence of biblical dissimulation? These concerns are well defined. In the apocryphal gospel of Nicodemus, priests say, "...If Jesus is remembered after fifty years, he will reign forever and create for himself a new people." (1) Paul suggests that studying genealogies is to be eschewed as leading to debate (I Tim 1:4, Tit 3:9) (Rome burned the genealogies in the temple (2)), and additionally that doubters are to be received, but not debated endlessly (Rom 14:1). Thomas, the quintessential doubter (Jn 20:29), was gently chastised for his disbelief, while shortly thereafter, heresiologists were leading pogroms against those who believed the Holy Spirit to proceed from the father, rather than from the father and son. Finally, to non-believers strong in their convictions, Paul suggests if anyone proves Christianity wrong, Christians deserve pity (I Cor 15:19 NIV), rather than being asked to re-evaluate beliefs and actions in light of history.

Sources

Preamble

(1) Any Woody Allen flick or A Space Odyssey (1968)

(2) Quantum physics; Copenhagen interpretation (Neils Bohr)

(3) Milgram experiment tested how much pain the average person would be willing to give another by an electric shock when asked to do so by an authorized authority. Experimenters did not tell the subjects that the recipients of the pain were actors. There still exists some question as to the morality of the experiment.

(4) Insurance Journal Nov 19, 2007, $800000 Settlement Approved in Mont. Psychologist Malpractice Case

(5) Archdiocese of Atlanta ~April 2004 - Selected three priests and three of the laity to serve on a board. One of the laymen quit citing the church's refusal to suggest that parents contact the police immediately as her reason for demitting. Article from Atlanta Journal-Constitution on Sally Horan.

5a) Catholic Church Lobbies Against Allowing More Sex Abuse Suits, June 20, 2012, New Yorker Magazine Margaret Hartman

(6) Pope John Paul II

(7) Enforced illiteracy - Nestorius

    I Cor 8:1 per Eisenman, James the Brother of Jesus 1997 p651

      – knowledge "puffs-up," love "builds-up."

    Ecc 12:12 per Brophy, Diana (Atlanta, GA) ~1992

      - much study is a weariness of the flesh.

    Understanding the Bible, John A. Buehrens 2003 p23

      - translating into the vernacular forbidden as challenging authority.

(8) Fr Mike - St. Michael's, Woodstock, GA ~ 2004

(9) Catholic Education Resource Center - The Crusades - Paul Crawford

(10) Catholic Truth, Catholic Bible - The Catholic Church is the only proper authority to consult in matters pertaining to the Bible.

"Empty your minds of secular knowledge" - John Chrysostom (307-407 Constantinople)

(11) Luther 1517. Ninety-five thesis nailed to the door of the Vatican.

(12) Fr Mike - St. Michael's, Woodstock, GA ~ 2004

Part I

   (1) Josephus, Antiquities 15.6.2 - innovations

   (2) John Briley, Gandhi 1982 movie – sews own clothes to avoid government control

   (3) Who Wrote the New Testament? Burton L. Mack 1995

      p43 – Perfect kingdom to which anyone can belong.

      P217 – Gnostics of John experience the new light and life.

   Josephus, Wars 2.8.3 – despisers of riches

Chapter I – The Power of Rome

   (1) Eisenman, James the Brother of Jesus, 1997 p28

   (2 & 3) Josephus - Wars 6.6.1

   (4) Eisenman, The New Testament Code 2006 p54

   (5) Josephus – Wars 7.10

   (6) The Ancient Historians, Michael Grant 1970 p147 – Rome destroys Corinth

   (7) The Ancient Historians, Michael Grant 1970 p217

[Rome's destruction - Eisenman, James the Brother of Jesus 1997 p50]

   (8) Essentials of World History, Jean Reeder Smith and Lacey Baldwin Smith 1980 p57

   (9) Josephus, Antiquities 14.12.2 (Cassius at Phillipi)

   (10) Josephus – Wars 1.4.3.4 (wives & children), 6, 3.7.36, 3.10.10 …

   (11) Eisenman, James the Brother of Jesus 1997 p27

   (12) Eisenman, James the Brother of Jesus 1997 pXXII

   (13) Eisenman, James the Brother of Jesus 1997 p50

Chapter II: Christianity – Removing Jewish Authority: The New Covenant

   (1) Byblos – "Book" in Greek.

   (2) Eisenman 1997, James, the Brother of Jesus p776

   (3) Marcus Jewish Community Center of Atlanta ~2002 … During an ecumenical discussion of Dan Brown's Blood.

   (4) Eisenman 2006, The New Testament Code p297 – Reversing … meaning.

(5) Kehillat and other Atlanta Synagogues have a plate of skullcaps in case you've forgotten yours (~1999).

(6) Eisenman, The New Testament Code 2006 p506

(7) Eisenman, James, the Brother of Jesus 1997 p102

    Eisenman, The New Tesatament Code 2006 p872

(8) Eisenman, The New Testament Code 2006 p29

(9) Eisenman, The New Testament Code p376,377

    <Dogs don't discern between clean and unclean>

(10) Josephus, Antiquities 9.14.3

(11) Yes, there are other differences between Mt and Lk, including differences in the lineage between Moses and David. Yes, the Jewish prophecy has the child born of a "young woman" rather than "virgin" (Is 7:14). Intro to "Snatch" 2000 – Brad Pitt.

(12) Catholic Encyclopedia – or any Roman Catholic person

(13) Josephus, Antiquities 3.1.7 (whole Law is only in the temple)

Chapter III – Caesar's Coin

1) There are those who will carry no coin, `nor carry or look on any graven image` - p826 James, the Brother of Jesus, Robert Eisenman 1997

2) Jesus' group had Judas who carried the purse (Jn 12:4-6, 13:29)

    Eisenman, The Dead Sea Scrolls and the First Christians:

        idols of silver and … gold p128

        no coins have yet been found in Qumran p98

        early Christians in Palestine … kept a common purse p102

            [were against Riches and class distinctions]

        Thou shalt not put a foreigner above you p224

            [The Temple Scroll: polluted offerings]

    Eisenman, James, the Brother of Jesus 1998

        Discussion of coins found at Qumran p88 - p90

        Essene-style, did not carry coins on his person p717

3) Eisenman, The New Testament Code 2006 p382

   Ban on Gentiles and gifts

   Eisenman, James, The Brother of Jesus 1997 p625

   Per Eisenman, the Mishna says when Herod Agrippa came to the Deuteronomic King Law, he teared up. Accommodating Pharisees shouted: You are our brother! three times. To me, these were either recognizing Herod's Maccabean ancestry against his family's behavior, Edomite ancestry or marriage to his new Maccabean wife as close enough, or performing some magic ritual.

(4) Josephus, Antiquities 14.4.4 (Pompey), Wars 6.2.4 (Titus)

   preserve the temple treasure as holy

5) The temple at Jerusalem serve as ... the center of a Jewish Banking network" p149 Who Wrote the New Testament, Burton L. Mack 1995

(6) Josephus, Wars 2.16.5

   Agrippa: You have not paid the tribute due Caesar

(7) Eisenman, The Dead Sea Scrolls and the First Christians 2004 p193

   Acceptance of sacrifices and gifts

Chapter IV – Rome's Authority According to Paul

   (1) Eisenman, James, the Brother of Jesus 1997 p24

   (2) Eisenman, James, the Brother of Jesus 1997 p742

Part II: Anomalies

Chapter V – Dating the Bible

   (1 & 2) Josephus - Antiquities Chapters 16 - 18 (Death of Herod followed by Census of Cyrenius of Syria

   (3) Josephus - Antiquities 18.5.2

   (4) Josephus - Antiquities 18.5.1, 18.5.4, 17.10.9

   (5) John the Baptist/Aretas/Jews/Philip vs. Herod: Josephus - Antiquities 18.5.2

      Herod/Philip scrapping over Herodias: Eisenman, James, the Brother of Jesus 1997 p108, 333

John/Aretas/Jews/Philip vs. Herod: p20 The New Testament Code, Robert Eisenman 2006

(6) Eisenman, James, the Brother of Jesus 1997 Chronological Charts

(7) Acharya S - The Christ Conspiracy p41

(8) Josephus - Antiquities does record an earthquake 15.15.2 in 31 BCE.

(9) Josephus - Antiquities records a lunar eclipse 17.6.4 March 13th 4BCE.

Footnote: No other eclipses recorded by Josephus.

(10) Josephus - Antiquities 18.5.2

(11) Marc Antony ruled the Eastern Roman Empire, including Syria.

Josephus - Antiquities 15.4.1

Grant, Michael - The Ancient Historians p217, p230

(12) Josephus - Antiquities 20.5.2

(13) Battle of Philippi

(14) Josephus - Wars 3.3.8

(15) Eisenman, James the Brother of Jesus 1997 p965

Eisenman, James the Brother of Jesus 1997 p798

(16) Eisenman - James the Brother of Jesus - Chronological Charts (Festus 60-62)

(17) Josephus - Antiquities 20.9.1

(18) Eisenman, James the Brother of Jesus 1997 p303

(19) Josephus - Antiquities 20.10.3

(20) James the Brother of Jesus - p781

Chapter VI – The Geography

(1) Hammond - Atlas of the Bible Lands p5, p422 James, the Brother of Jesus, Robert Eisenman 1997

(2) Acharya S - The Christ Conspiracy p39

(3) Josephus - Wars 2.20-22

(4) Eisenman - James, the Brother of Jesus p244

Chapter VII – Ethiopian History

   (1) Eisenman – James, the Brother of Jesus p917

   (2) Eisenman - The New Testament Code p76-78

   (3) Eisenman – The New Testament Code p76-77

   (4) Josephus - Antiquities 4.8.40

      Eisenman, James, the Brother of Jesus 1997 p922

   (5) Eisenman - The New Testament Code p952-953

Chapter VIII – Misquoting Jewish Scripture

   (1) Eisenman - James, the Brother of Jesus 1997 p224

IX - Jewish history per Stephen (Paul's authority)

   (1) Eisenman - James, the Brother of Jesus 1997 p303, 609

   (2) Shortell, Ray – Understanding the Bible 2012

   (3) Eisenman - James, the Brother of Jesus 1997 p530

   (4) Eisenman - James, the Brother of Jesus 1997 p184

   (5) Eisenman - James, the Brother of Jesus 1997 p609

Part III: Theology

Chapter X: Meditation on the silence of Jesus

Chapter XI: Moses and Prophets

   (1) Mainly documenting itself, but...

   101 Myths of the Bible

   The Christ Conspiracy 1999 S.Acharya p90

      -combined with other documents

   Sefer Yetzirah 1997 Aryeh Kaplan pXV

      -last books put together at the second temple

   The Denver Catholic Biblical School Program 1994 p75, 76, 77

Men like the priest made a tremendous effort to collect the various religious writings they had been able to rescue from the conflagration of Jerusalem, edit and combine them into a great account of their sacred history that could inspire them to faithfulness even in the times of the Exile.

...The old sacred stories that had been passed down by word of mouth in every tribe for generations...

...It may well be that D actually wrote down these traditional laws, which had evolved out of centuries of experience, only after the defeat of the northern kingdom, when they were no longer the official law of the land.

P thought the most important thing he had to work with was the accumulated traditions of the Jerusalem priesthood, which he had been taught since childhood, of which he had some written records, and about which he could consult his fellow priests in exile.

The Age of Reason, Thomas Paine 1796 Gramercy 1993 p133

(2) The Denver Catholic Biblical School Program 1994 p74, p77

101 Myths of the Bible Gary Greenberg 2000 xvi – xx

(3) The Christ Conspiracy S.Aracha 1999 p340

(4) The Christ Conspiracy S.Aracha 1999 p119

(5) Eisenman, James, the Brother of Jesus p114

(6) St. Maria Goretti (Italy murder of girl and church in Coal Valley Il. 1985)

(7) The Ancient Historians, Michael Grant 1970 p23

(8) Babylon Never Conquered Egypt, Cary Cook 11/7/13

http://www.sanityquestpublishing.com/essays/BabEgypt.html

c.567	HOPHRA, now working for Babylonians with Babylonian army, attacks AHMOSE-II, and routs his Ionian mercenaries.
c.566	AHMOSE-II defeats Babylonian invasion of Egypt. Former pharaoh Hophra is captured by Egyptians. Sources conflict on whether he is executed or allowed to live. No further Babylonian attempts on Egypt are recorded.

(9) Taught as promoting arguing with deity in some Jewish circles.

(10) Josephus Antiquities 3.1.7-38, 3.5.4-90

(11) The New Testament Code, Eisenman 2006 p723

(12) The New Testament Code Eisenman 2006 p866

(13) Josephus, Wars 7.9

(14) 101 Myths of the Bible Gary Greenberg 2000 xvi

Part IV: James v Paul

Chapter XII – Cosmopolitan Paul v Jewish James (take one)

  (1) Eisenman - James, the Brother of Jesus pXX

  (2) Eisenman – James, the Brother of Jesus p303

  (3) James enters Holy of Holies - Eisenman - James the Brother of Jesus p344

  (4) Eisenman - James the Brother of Jesus pXX

  (5) Eisenman, James the Brother of Jesus 1997 p352

Chapter XIII – Circumcision (Paul v James take two)

  (1) Eisenman, The New Testament Code p76-78

  (2) Eisenman, James, the Brother of Jesus p695

Chapter XIV – SuperApostles (Paul v James take three)

  (1) Eisenman, The New Testament Code 1997 p605

Chapter XV – The Letter of the Law (Paul v James take five)

  (1) Eisenman, James, the Brother of Jesus 1997 p600

Chapter XVI – Gospels are Secondary Resources

  (1) Bible study teacher from long ago…

    The One-stop Bible Guide, Mike Beaumont 2006 p73

      The good news was communicated initially by word of mouth.

      Jews were taught from childhood to remember oral material accurately

      and Jesus style made it all the more easy.

    A History of Christ, Paul Johnson 1976

      …the progressive elimination of the first generation death provided in the sixties

      an urgent incentive to record Jesus' teaching in imperishable shape.

Chapter XVII – Robbing Peter to Pay Paul

  (1) Arachya S - The Christ Conspiracy p32

  (2) Eisenman, James, the Brother of Jesus p350-352

    "Demythologizing Peter"

(3) Eisenman, James, the Brother of Jesus 1997 p120

(4) The NAB Catholic Serendipity Bible, Zondervan 1999 p1698

(5) Eisenman, James, the Brother of Jesus 1997 p651

(6) Eisenman, James, the Brother of Jesus 1997 pXXX

(7) Eisenman, James, the Brother of Jesus 1997 p544-547

Chapter XVIII – Peaceful James v Rabble-Rousing Pau

(1) Eisenman, James, the Brother of Jesus 1997 p962

(2) Josephus, Ant 20.9.1

    Eisenman, The New Testament Code 2006 p60

(3) Eisenman, James, the Brother of Jesus 1997 p320

(4) Josephus - Antiquities 18.5.2

    Eisenman, James, the Brother of Jesus 1997 p342

(5) Eisenman, James, the Brother of Jesus 1997 p962

Chapter XIX – The Family of James (Priestly?)

(1) Eisenman, James, the Brother of Jesus 1997 p924 – 925

(2) Eisenman, James, the Brother of Jesus 1997 p770-771, 917

(3) Eisenman, James, the Brother of Jesus 1997 p96

(4) Eisenman, the New Testament Code 2006 p602

(5) Eisenman, James, the Brother of Jesus 1997 p819

(6) Eisenman, James, the Brother of Jesus 1997 p666

(7) Patterson, Robinson & Bethge The Fifth Gospel 1998 p7

(8) Barnstone, The Other Bible 1984 Acts of Thomas p469

(9) Eisenman, James, the Brother of Jesus 1997 p117

(10) Eisenman, James, the Brother of Jesus 1997 p183-184

(11) Eisenman, James, the Brother of Jesus 1997 p689

(12) Eisenman, James the Brother of Jesus 1997 p689

(13) Eisenman, James, the Brother of Jesus 1997 p847

(14) Eisenman, James the Brother of Jesus 1997 p847,413

Chapter XX – The Family of Paul (Herodian?)

  (1) Eisenman, The New Testament Code 2006

       Chapter: Paul as Herodian - p504

  (2) Josephus, Antiquities 20.1.1

  (3) Josephus, Antiquities 20.9.4

  (4) Eisenman, the New Testament Code 2006 p504

  (5) Arnold Fruchtenbaum, Commentary on Acts

      Corinth, Paul before Gallio Section 12a

      "Gallio was born in Cordova in Spain in 3BC."

  (5) Eisenman, James, the Brother of Jesus 1997 p962

  (6) Eisenman, James, the Brother of Jesus 1997 p638-639

Part V: Summary

Chapter XXI – The Power of Rome through History

  (1) Eisenman, James, the Brother of Jesus 1997 p122,462

  (2) Eisenman, James, the Brother of Jesus 1997 p601, 917

  (3) Eisenman, James, the Brother of Jesus 1997 p207

  (4) Eisenman, James the Brother of Jesus 1997 pXXX

  (5) Fr Mike, St. Michael's Woodstock, GA ~2004

  (6) Settle it therefore in your hearts, not to meditate before what ye shall answer Lk 21:14

    …the testimony of the Lord is sure; making wise the simple. Ps 19:11

    Of the making of many books there is no end… Ec 12:12

    Many of them … brought their books together and burned them… Ac 18:19

  (7) Mormon at Waffle House corner of 400 & 53 ~1995

  (8) Acquaintance struggled with his Mormonism ~1996

  (9) Fr. Mike, St. Michael's Woodstock ~2007 – humility and obedience

    - quoted in its entirety in the preamble

  (10) Eisenman, James the Brother of Jesus 1997 p344

XXII - The Cup of Blood

(1) Eisenman, James the Brother of Jesus 1997 p222, 151

(2) Eisenman, James, the Brother of Jesus 1997 p814,374-375, 244-245, 243

(3) Eisenman, James, the Brother of Jesus 1997 p21

(4) Eisenman, The New Testament Code 2006 p935

(5) Eisenman, James, the Brother of Jesus 1997 p922

<uncanny control over the material>

<understood what they were doing>

Eisenman, The New Testament Code 2006 p612, 297

<bowdlerized>

(6) S. Achaya The Christ Conspiracy 1999 p32

(7) Eisenman, James, the Brother of Jesus 1997 p963

(8) Eisenman, The New Testament Code 2006 p484

(9) Eisenman, James, the Brother of Jesus 1997 p284

(10) Eisenman, The New Testament Code 2006 p485

(11) Shortell, Understanding the Bible

(12) Shortell, Understanding the Bible

(13) Shortell, Understanding the Bible

(14) Eisenman, James the Brother of Jesus 1997 p636-637

Eisenman, The New Testament Code 2006 p932, 710-711

(15) Shortell, Understanding the Bible

(16) Shortell, Understanding the Bible

Postscripts:

Gospel Anomalies:

(1) Josephus Antiquities 15.11.6

(2) James, the Brother of Jesus, Eisenman p442

(3) Shortell, Understanding the Bible - 2012

(4) S.Acharya The Christ Conspiracy 1999 p205 <on a holiday?>

(5) Time Benedict XVI: Jews not to blame for Jesus death March 3, 2011

– Excerpts from Jesus of Nazareth: Holy Week

Postscript: Failed Prophesies (Messianic, Judah):

(1) 101 Myths of the Bible, Gary Greenberg 2000 Myth 99

(2) The Dead Sea Scrolls and the First Christians, 1996 Eisenman, p36

"'Ezra and Nehemiah make it clear that many of the priestly clans returning from exile could not prove their genealogies and some were not priests at all." Robert Eisenman, James the Brother of Jesus 1997 p381

Other `Sadducees,` epitomized by Judas Maccabee, are consistently more resistance-minded, xenophobic, non-accommodating, zealous for the law, following a Phineas-minded approach to Ezekiel's Zadokite Covenant. It should be recalled Phineas won for himself and his descendants by killing backsliders introducing foreigners and pollution into the camp of Israel. ibid

Personal Note: Astrology in the Bible

(1) Linda Goodman, Linda Goodman's Love Signs pg13

Shortell, Ray Poetry Corner - Oracle 20/20 Feb 2006 pg30

S.Achaya The Christ Conspiracy 1999 pg113

Brophy, Diane: I Cor 13 (Atlanta, GA) ~1992

(2) Josephus, Antiquities 3.7.7 – Twelve signs

(3) Josephus, Antiquities 3.3.7 – Veil

Postscript: The teachings of Jesus – the whole of the law

(1) James, the Brother of Jesus, Robert Eisenman 1997 p83

Postscript: Hebrew Scriptural Issues

(1) Darius was the father of Xerxes, not the other way around (Dan 9:1)

Grant, Michael, The Ancient Historians 1970 p24

(2) Jer 20:4 – All Judah to be delivered to Babylon or killed

24:8-10 – Jewish Zedekiah and remnant in Egypt to disappear from the land

29:16-18 – Jews not in Babylon to be banished

42:10- non-Babylonian Jews begged to remain in Judah but flee to Egypt

44:28 – Jewish remnant in Egypt to return a few

(3) Eisenman, The New Testament Code 2006 p376

Contemporaneous Religions:

(1) Fishing Trip, KY ~02 – Dan Walker

(2) The Christ Conspiracy, Acharya S. 1999 p154, 205

Millennial Reign:

(1) Eisenman, The New Testament Code 2006 p297

Final Note:

    (1) The Other Bible – Willis Barnstone – 1984 p374

    (2) Josephus The Complete Works – translated by William Whiston – 1998

    (2) p929 accuracy ended at the destruction of Jerusalem

    (2) 6.6.4 – set fire to the repository of the archives

About the Author:

    (1) Eisenman, James the Brother of Jesus 1997 p651

    (2) Eisenman, James the Brother of Jesus 1997 p176

    (3) Eisenman, James the Brother of Jesus 1997 p651

Bibliography

    James, The Brother of Jesus, Robert Eisenman 1997

    The New Testament Code, Robert Eisenman 2006

    101 Myths of the Bible, Gary Greenburg 2000

The Christ Conspiracy, Acharya S. 1999

Who Wrote the New Testament? Burton L. Mack 1995

Josephus The Complete Works – translated by William Whiston 1998

The Denver Catholic Biblical School Program 1994

The Other Bible, Barnstone 1984 <Apocrypha>

Fr. Mike, St. Michael's Woodstock, GA ~2004

Atlas of the Bible Lands, Hammond 1990 updated 2002

The Age of Reason, Thomas Paine 1790

The Ancient Historians, Michael Grant 1970

The Fifth Gospel, Patterson, Robinson, Bethge 1998 <Gospel of Thomas>

95 Thesis – Martin Luther – 1517 <Start of Protestantism>

Nestorius <Eastern Orthodox leader> … What does heresiology mean to you?

St. Maria Goretti <Roman Catholic Church> Coal Valley, IL 1974 – 2012

Mark Antony – Killed Caesar's assassins at Philippi, lost sea battle off Greece when Cleopatra fled, killed himself after her apparent suicide in Egypt <Josephus Antiq 15.4.1, Grant, Michael The Ancient Historians 1970>

Catholic Education Resource Center - The Crusades - Paul Crawford

<Four Myths About the Crusades, The Intercollegiate Review Spring 2001>

Sefer Yetzirah 1997 Aryeh Kaplan <Jewish philosophy>

Copenhagen Interpretation, Neils Bohr ~1920 <Quantum Physics, lack of empirical authority>

Milgram Experiment, Yale 1963 <psychology of authority>

Linda Goodman's Love Signs, Goodman 1991 <astrological personality development>

Archdiocese of Atlanta 2002 <sexual abuse policies>

Understanding the Bible, John A. Buehrens 2003 <ensuring my work is original>

Understanding the Bible, John R.W. Stott 1999 <ensuring my work is original>

Dan Walker, Indiana Fishing trip ~2002 <Hearsay Zoroastrianism>

Diane Brophy, Georgia colleague ~1993 <Ec 12:12, I Cor 13>

Courtney Williams, Georgia Kennesaw Sidelines ~2008 <Protestant Insight>

Bibles: KJV, Catholic Serendipity 1999, www.biblegateway.com

Suggested Reading

A History of God, Karen Armstrong 1994

Crucifixion and Turin Shroud Mysteries Revealed, Pierre Krijbolder 1999

Who Wrote the New Testament, Burton L. Mack 1989 <I cringe when proposing this last due to the author's repeated and flippant stating of unsupported and unhelpful opinion as fact>

About the Author:

Raised the Catholic son of a Catholic mother and Protestant father, went to the University of Illinois for a Degree in Computer Science, followed by twenty years as a healthcare programmer and physics master's dropout (Ga Tech & State) blaming long hours of bible study and a terrible commute from Alpharetta. The dedication to my nephew Jake is in the hopes that Jakie's time and devotion might be spent anywhere desired rather than required delving deeply into the multiple layers of meaning in the Bible due to its claim as being the key to life (Peter's keys, Mt 16:19). Diane Brophy's 1993 citations of I Cor 13, Ecc 12:12, and Ten Commandments long remained allowing me to connect commonalities from Astrology (Linda Goodman's Love Signs p13 and The Christ Conspiracy p113). Thanks to Elvin Frame, my bible study teacher from the Church of the Nazarene in Marietta, a neighbor, Jeff Peace, whose invaluable guidance led me to study James and upset a Priest and Rabbi at the Jewish community center in Dunwoody during an Ecumenical discussion of Dan Brown's works over the "Jerusalem Council" and why Hellenists would ever dispute against Paul (beg pardon). Note: My Catholic Serendipity Bible lists the description in its title for the passage, so if Catholic Priests don't want it called the Jerusalem Council and would prefer the family of James castigated once again, maybe y'all could just remove the header, which probably isn't in the original Greek rather than using it for authority in one context and claiming it doesn't exist in the next?

From my introductory quotes, you'll note that the church doesn't appreciate folks learning enough to handle a serious discussion. In The Age of Reason, Thomas Paine notes his concern from biblical reasoning, which we subsequently ignored: Paul's thesis in I Cor 8 could just as easily be a Marxist manifesto on the uselessness of knowledge. Fortunately, Dr. Eisenman's research found the key in the Damascus document, noting I Cor 8 as just one example of Paul's scorn for learning (1). Another example, in my opinion, is Paul's speaking in tongues (I Cor 14:6) probably referencing Pentecost. In contrast, James as probable "Mebakker" probably learned multiple languages in the usual way - Eisenman: "mastery over the secrets of men and their innumerable tongues" (2), "Righteous teacher in whose heart [resided] the knowledge to interpret … the prophets (3), which were only kept at the temple (Jos Ant 3.1.7 …that Scripture which is laid up in the temple, informs us…). James promotes learning and doing (Ja 1:25). While Paul and Jesus promote naïveté, Lk 21:14 - Settle it therefore in your hearts, not to meditate before what ye shall answer (Argh!!! The Bible directs us not to study and against knowledge).

As for the quote from Fr. Mike, whether the request was for Coptic or our Peshitta escapes me. However, as a personal response, after lengthy study, some of each of these languages has been learned. Latin was picked up singing old hymns in the Moline Boys Choir or conglomerated from Spanish, French, or Portuguese when needed (Tu no sabe nada! N'est ce pas? Como se disais "Castle" en Portuguese?) For Aramaic, there was "The Passion of the Christ" 2004, by the end of which you've learned a bit. There's a bit here and there for Hebrew from a language course, Western Mysticism, and Kaballah studies. For Greek, there are only a couple of words like philia, agape, eros, and even "evangelize," which I pulled from the Greek Scriptures based upon my knowledge of Greek pronunciation from physics and double-checked with a Greek friend against other biblical translations. For Coptic, I visited a church where they said the Bible was their documentation, too. For our Peshitta, an e-mail was sent to the authors explaining why the translation of Paul's body burned with fire needed to remain just so against another suggested and "preferred" translation. Dr. Eisenman also has a letter from me asking for a student to come speak locally. The point is that authority no longer resides with the church because we have several translations, that understanding can happen in the vernacular (Latin for `local tongue,` to which the Roman Catholic Church translated in the banner year of 1964), and that we should respect study as it truly builds-up (Acts 20:32).

www.ingramcontent.com/pod-product-compliance
Lightning Source LLC
Chambersburg PA
CBHW080351170426
43194CB00014B/2752